Ring-Tailed Lemurs

Victoria Blakemore

© 2017 Victoria Blakemore

All rights reserved. This book or parts thereof may not be reproduced in any form, stored in any retrieval system, or transmitted in any form by any means—electronic, mechanical, photocopy, recording, or otherwise—without prior written permission of the publisher, except as provided by United States of America copyright law. For permission requests, write to the publisher, at "Attention: Permissions Coordinator," at the address below.

vblakemore.author@gmail.com

Copyright info/picture credits

Cover, GUDKOV ANDREY/Shutterstock; Page 3, onkelramirez1/Pixabay; Page 5, webandi/Pixabay; Page 7, swecology/Pixabay; Page 9, MemoryCatcher/Pixabay; Pages 10-11, Seaq68/Pixabay; Page 13, Karsten_Kettermann/Pixabay; Page 15, Marcsi01/Pixabay; Page 17, koffergepackt/Pixabay; Page 19, Eelffica/Pixabay; Page 21, onkelramirez1/Pixabay; Page 23; stanvpetersen/Pixabay; Page 25, onkelramirez1/Pixabay; Page 27, Bart-ter-Haar/Pixabay; Page 29, onkelramirez1/Pixabay; Page 31, Elisabeth25/Pixabay; Page 33, GUDKOV ANDREY/Shutterstock

Table of Contents

What are Ring-Tailed Lemurs?	2
Size	4
Physical Characteristics	6
Habitat	8
Range	10
Diet	12
Communication	16
Movement	18
Young	20
Troop Life	22
Lifespan	24
Population	26
Ring-Tailed Lemurs in Danger	28
Helping Ring-Tailed Lemurs	30
Glossary	34

What Are Ring-Tailed Lemurs?

Ring-tailed lemurs are mammals. They are members of the primate family. Other primates include tarsiers, monkeys, and apes.

They are black, gray, and white and have a long, striped tail.

The name "ring-tailed" comes from the black and white rings on their tail.

Size

When fully grown, ring-tailed lemurs are usually between fifteen and eighteen inches long. Their tail can add another twenty to twenty-four inches.

Adults often weigh between four and five pounds.

Male and female ring-tailed lemurs are usually about the same size.

Physical Characteristics

Ring-tailed lemurs have a long tail. It can be used to help them balance as they move through the trees.

They have a thick coat of fur, which helps them to stay warm. It is thinner on their belly, so they can **absorb** heat from the sun.

Their paws are like hands and can be used for climbing and **grasping**.

Habitat

Ring-tailed lemurs live in forests and dry **scrublands**. They are sometimes found close to rivers.

They need places with lots of plants to eat and trees where they can hide from predators.

Range

Ring-tailed lemurs are only found in one place, the island of Madagascar in Africa.

Madagascar is home to many **unique** animals such chameleons, aye-ayes, and the fossa.

Diet

Ring-tailed lemurs are **classified** as **omnivores**. They eat meat and plants.

Their diet is mostly made up of fruit, but they also eat leaves, flowers, and bark. They may also eat insects and small animals such as chameleons.

Unlike many other primates, ring-tailed lemurs spend a lot of time on the ground. They look for food there.

Ring-tailed lemurs play an important role in their habitat. They eat a lot of fruit and spread the seeds through their **waste**.

As they spread the fruit seeds to different places, new plants are able to grow. They provide food for many other animals.

Ring-tailed lemurs eat a lot when food is available. It helps them to survive later when food may be **scarce**.

15

Communication

Lemurs have a special scent gland on their wrists. They use this scent to keep other lemurs away from their **territory**.

They rub their tail on the scent glands to make it smell, then wave it at the other lemur in what is called a "stink fight."

Ring-tailed lemurs use sound to communicate with each other and warn about predators that are nearby.

Movement

Ring-tailed lemurs spend about half of their time on the ground. They walk or run on all four legs, with their tail standing straight up behind them.

They have been **observed** running at speeds of about twelve miles per hour.

Ring-tailed lemurs are able to run along tree branches and leap between trees.

Young Ring-Tailed Lemurs

Ring-tailed lemurs usually have one baby. When it is first born, it drinks it's mother's milk.

Groups of ring-tailed lemurs work together to take care of young lemurs. This allows the mothers time to rest and find food for themselves.

Babies hang on to their mother's chest and back until they are old enough to climb on their own.

Troop Life

Ring-tailed lemurs are social animals. They live in groups that are called troops. A troop usually has about fifteen lemurs, but may have as many as thirty.

Troops are usually led by the oldest female lemur. She gets first choice of the available food.

Ring-tailed lemurs are often seen sitting or laying in the sun. The thin hair on their bellies allows them to **absorb** heat.

Grooming

Ring-tailed lemurs have special teeth that are called their "dental comb." They use them to groom their fur and the fur of other lemurs.

They are often seen in pairs, grooming each other at the same time.

Ring-tailed lemurs lick and bite at their fur to keep it clean and free from pests.

Population

Ring-tailed lemurs are **endangered**. There are not many left in the wild. If their population continues to **decline**, they could become **extinct**.

There are believed to be less than 2,500 ring-tailed lemurs left in the wild.

Ring-tailed lemurs usually live between sixteen and nineteen years in the wild.

Ring-Tailed Lemurs in Danger

Ring-tailed lemurs are facing two main threats: habitat loss and hunting.

Habitats are being cut down and cleared for farmland, buildings, and roads. It can be hard for ring-tailed lemurs to find a safe place to live.

In some places, ring-tailed lemurs are hunted for food. They are also taken from the wild to be kept as pets.

Helping Ring-Tailed Lemurs

Special **preserves** in Madagascar provide animals like ring-tailed lemurs with a safe habitat.

There are laws that prevent ring-tailed lemurs from being hunted and trapped. These laws are there to keep lemurs safe in their natural habitats.

Researchers are studying ring-tailed lemur populations to learn more about them. They hope to be able to find more ways to help.

Some groups are focusing on education. They want to teach people about ring-tailed lemurs. They hope people will want to help.

Glossary

Absorb: to take in

Classified: put into groups or classes

Decline: get smaller, decrease

Endangered: at risk of becoming extinct

Extinct: when there are no more of an animal left in the wild

Grasping: holding on to

Observed: seen or noticed

Omnivore: an animal that eats meat and plants

Preserves: areas of land set up to protect plants and animals

Scarce: hard to find, not much available

Scrublands: land that has lots of grasses, bushes, and low plants

Territory: an area of land that an animal claims as its own

Unique: different, unusual

Waste: material given off by the body after food is digested

About the Author

Victoria Blakemore is a first grade teacher in Southwest Florida with a passion for reading.

You can visit her at

www.elementaryexplorers.com

Also in This Series

Also in This Series